What Of Us Remains

Other works by Eric Williamson

Miscreant Issue Zero

When We Were The Voyage

Strange Worlds

Chapbook Series

This Is Our Secret

What Of Us Remains

What Of Us Remains

chapbook series II

Eric Williamson

What Of Us Remains

Copyright 2023 © Eric Williamson

Cover Design by Marco Fontanili

ISBN: 979-8-218-28429-9

CONTENTS

What Of Us Remains

WHAT IS WRONG WITH US NOW?

We haven't always been here, but we have.

We haven't always had this escape, but we hid.

Climbing the apartment steps with an empty key ring

the future has beckoned, and you are locked.

There are molecules so hardened the sun cannot divide.

We talk flowers into contusions.

We are discrete while lassoing silence.

How best are you to be trusted

holding operating instructions to dating in limp hands?

I have been in this lowland between hills and mountains once

which to you is more than a hundred times.

The minute-hand shelters the hour.

You are not sure what you are doing.

We are compelled to be good to each other and bad

and spend precious time biting our lips before we speak.

You saw your life dangling like young in jaws.

And the universe, like everything, flies apart.

The second-hand stops for a second.

What we have built crumbles down in our minds.

We are left with what washes up on the shore.

And I alone circle the beach,

the hungry peregrine soaring on his own revelation.

You're as young as you'll ever be.

Maybe you won't make another mistake.

It's the sighing stars that turn their faces away.

This time is yours and not yours alone.

AMNESIA

And swiftly

    the shadows silenced

    irrevocably

    like the artifacts in museums

behind reinforced glass,

with blurred, unfocused eyes,

    like love letters and calculations

    in photographs.

BLACK MOOD

can i interrupt your thoughts?

can i urge you to accept this gentleness?

            and be content?

you seem to be struggling for an answer

features acute with self-disgust

smile lost, replaced with that sober calm

            resembling regret

i wore a grin like a smirk

caught up in the balancing

devoid of will or intent or desire

the fear in that moment of what i've become

the years of unconscious shaping

      molding — unaware, passive

was that stint of rebellion awareness

      or pre-programmed sculpting

you were poised between consciousness

and abandonment

native impulses

to take all harm upon yourself

the powerlessness and its defense

the source from which it arose

i regret the interruption

your thoughts? i urge you

DIRECTIONLESS

Having lost sight

of the highway signs

and reflective markers

that gauge

and space

you and I

in the blurring

of landscapes

and the speeding

catastrophes.

OVERRIPE

perfume and sweat

melons ripe to burst

peaches and pomegranates

nightshade and moonbloom

sweet treats cascade

Lazarus is still walking

THE VACANCY

steam fogs the mirror

a nervous marine layer

while the tub faucet sizzles

her thin fingers splay

run down the glass

for a minute, maybe longer

four vertical lines pierce the clouds

four lines stretch like prison bars

her face visible from behind

the vacant eyes not quite matching up

she can feel the veins

in her neck pulse

she can feel the warm tiles

beneath her feet

quivering legs losing balance

her nightgown clings

to her breasts like something familiar

something missing

she could not have fathomed

that her child

would turn blue so fast

and downstairs the phone rings

as water overspills

and floods the house

INSIGHT

What gets into me

Must be you

If wisdom comes with age

Then I have no clue

And Then the Scene Shifts

And then the scene shifts to her desk, the photograph of him

One firm-knuckled grasp wrapping a rusty bicycle handlebar

His coy small-mouthed dimples hyphen the end of one sentence

And the beginning of another

The bicycle is frozen in advance

Pedals stationary and lasting,

Knees angled outward, bookmarking movement

With perpetual unwavering balance, he is leaning back listless

His other hand and arm upraised and flared

Palm pitched leeward and gaining breeze

Skyrockets towards the frame

That ensconces with thick beechwood and blanched cardboard matte

As if he could grab it and pull himself out

This photograph upon her desk is one of many where he is captured

This photograph is one of many where he is a second from peace

This photograph is one of many that cuts her like steel

A dog barks, a cat mewls, she awakens still wavering

Before his photograph upon her desk

She muffles before turning it down, and with a sigh

Paperclips herself over her bed, toe-tips touching the floor

She reaches for a stack of disheveled glossies

Music soft and gently redeeming, blue jazz, blankets her background

And envelops her as familiar mistrusting arms.

There is a place called discipline where marks are given for giving up

They are not medals or ribbons, or embossed certificates

They are not proclamations, dedications, or trite bequeaths

They simply are

And then the scene shifts to his desk, the photograph of her

ANOTHER THEORY FOR EVOLUTION

I think of Occam's Razor, which states;

"The best theory is the one requiring the fewest modifications

In order to fit the available observations." Or, in other words,

"The simplest answer is probably the right one."

And, I think I like the way that sounds. I think of rituals.

The kind that brings about a soothing, calm, almost meditative

State of bliss. I think of your feet and your smooth

Angular toes and arches, and the ritual love bathing

When they rest in my palm. And like a river rock resting

In the running waters of a hidden recess, I glide over you.

I think of horizons. That infinite point where land meets sky

And they kiss. I think how mountain peaks rise, all jagged

And purposeful, to penetrate the sky. And how the whole time

The sky just wraps her arms around and loves.

And, I think I like the way that sounds. I smile when I think

Of paraffin. How the idea alone, of us two on our knees

In the snow with hot wax, hunched over with only our hands
and lips

To shape the molds, sounds so spiritual. We fill the molds

And magically separate our fruits.

Later, I'll think of us wrapped in the solace of each other's
arms.

And the shadow play we'll weave with fingers entwined

In light from those candles. And of Gustav Klimt.

The words *layered* & *perfection* mirror the sight of

The Kiss. Le Baiser. I think of the angularity

Of masculinity and her feminine circles in cycles. And the fish

Moving through her. The sea. The sky. Then evolution.

How we have since shed skins. Casting off wings that alone

Only got us high. And, since swimming, never gotten us as
deep.

To Whom It May Concern, In Regards To...

He awoke at the docks aware of losing

& what was lost & at the same moment

Starving. Again, he awoke & recalled

Something about touch & the consequence

Of lack of. (She thought in terms of circles.

He, in straight lines.) He dreamt of that winter.

Nights so cold sap would freeze & trees would burst.

Air sharp enough 2 shatter & that whine,

Hypnotizing, of warped wood being split wide.

Akin 2 failure, as a stuttering

Panhandler, he misplaced the ability

2 enjoy classical literature,

Literally. Everything is metaphor,

An implied comparison, even Ariadne

Holding the thread for Theseus in the

Minotaur's maze—"Woman Grounds Sanity

For Man, Lost" —searching for what is always

Behind him. Orpheus & Eurydice.

"Sinister," highlighted against his bike.

Waiting at the bus stop because he is

Touch starved & has a crush & a nameless

Cafeteria worker did enlighten

Him w/ an unconscious, passing back-rub.

New to the practice of patience, whispers

Imply a shout, implies a full-moon howl!

He will try. Oh, how he will try! Yet he

Wonders which become doubt, and hope is fear.

Last night he dreamt the dream. The exact 1

That he had dreamt the night before & it

Literally, dealt w/ him, Theseus

& Ariadne & Minotaur's maze.

Yet, this time, Ariadne wouldn't stay

Put. She followed Theseus silently

& instead of holding the thread, she tied

Knots in it & then stuffed them in her mouth.

Unmistakably yours, E. Williamson

CHISHANGO

Dear E,

Drinking Elephant beer in Tucson. Beside the roll of film

are pictures, me, 17 May 1997, me

shooing a fly, government buildings,

the view out my back door, waterfall, Mulanje.

Newspaper rentals stain my fingers, and I am not behaving.

I was not wearing underwear, and you could smell it on us,

the sex, the stench, when once it was mysterious,

when once something good, when my commitment wasn't an

accident.

A sad commitment there on a Greyhound bus

when blue-eyed angels slept and I touched your cheek

to my tongue. Days when beauty hurt like a presence

people envy, or 1979, when the skin from my bare toe was

scalloped in bicycle spokes. K, let's move in together.

Dancing faster and faster, cocooning the lies.

You never knew these things I tell you know. I saw friends

each night you weren't around, Prozac girl, failed dates,

and "just friends" from out of town.

I numbered these traps as they shuffled by,

this little white girl in red shoes, no smile.

Julius threw plates and stained walls, stripping paint.

Yes, I lived

each night you weren't around. Never showed you my words,

words you never read. But, you know not these things.

You don't even know now.

Tonight I remind myself. I wore that sweater, scent and filth,
for days

back when there was a reason. Foolish and sentimental, I'll
touch a wildflower

to my eye, and recall how dad said you could eat all, but that.

How I could've watched you forever,

fifty cents in my pocket, a candle in my hand.

You've since sent me gloves, one month ago today. I simply smile,

slipping them on like fur from a squirrel, down on knees

shifting my compost pile.

My garden nearly dead, and the road out of Chitipa empty.

For no headlights nor streetlamps dot the midnight roads in this country,

and under my stars, coyote-boy, you stand in the midst

and sigh looking for wings, forbidden to fly.

While your photo is a shield smiling from beside my bed

I want you to know I haven't lost my feet, and

I never think of you at all.

xK

TIMEPIECE

I must admit I respected you

for less than I should.

You were the woman who spoke to me

through the radio

at night

a child's station

stories and actors replacing the cuddle

of aftermath quivering.

Pressing my penis into your back

legs wrapping halfway around

your fetal fold

is a draping arm lapping in and out

of conscious and sub-desire.

Those flannel sheets that scorched tender flesh

in flannel patterns of stripes that strip

and subtle raw-chin grinding neck.

I must admit I respected you

far more than I should.

A leather caressed timepiece

this watch tugging at my waist.

You gave to moments a designation like a child

whose hands dig for the piece

of candy, treasure bespoke in quarters,

snapshots and days that revolve in thoughtful

elegance.

A subtle giving

in such taking. For that I feel

without asking

taking this moment now of me

how so much

you are like time. Passing. Passing.

Living. Taking. Gone.

Ask much of all that it is I can give.

For you are minutes, hours,

breath in stale winter

mist. Fog sheathed Sound crept

into them over a heart

left unknowing

the child's voice of its own story

before sleep is taped anew

only to resume.

DRY INK

wire-rim, turquoise-tinted Lennon shades adorn

a fallen angel whose tattered wings finally expose

open diaries now at rest

atop curved seashells glued to a cardboard box

near the empty footlocker and it's broken lock

Can you remember our music, my Beauty?

Panasonic stereo serenades in elusive beats

our instrument's ancient melody in accompaniment

burning incense and the scent of bared skin

intense sensations flower a climax never to last

your snicker, and my sigh, never again have I

weathered drywall and chipped paint settle over

crushed cigarette butts and snowflake ashes

amidst patchwork carpet

Christmas lights and soiled ebony sheets ascent

labeled soda cans pinning down the remains of

your piled letters of dried ink

INNOCENCE LOST

i remember a time of simple innocence

not necessarily part of it

but i remember the cadence

i can recall images of a boy, near a stream

not necessarily me

but maybe a part of someone else

i can imagine the aroma of dandelions

not necessarily the pride

but definitely the scent

i can remember an age of discovery

not necessarily a specific date

but i remember the moment

i can recall feeling a girl, on the ground

not necessarily you

but maybe a part of something wonderful

i can imagine the taste of cotton

not necessarily the guilt

but definitely the smoked weed

i can remember a day of expectations

not necessarily of what

but i remember the feeling

i can recall caressing a breast, under a bridge

not necessarily the nipple

but maybe it was that angelic

i can imagine the desire of longing

not necessarily the stumble

but maybe a part of the boy left behind

near a stream, on the ground, under a bridge

CAFETERIA

There is a laminate table we sit at.

Condiments anxiously rest in their prison cells.

Our lunchroom platters nearly touch

as we pick at the food

which lay eager for consumption.

We sit next to each other and we talk.

And though we do not see the glow,

the filaments of light,

dancing around us,

the five rest at the table whisper

to themselves, transfixed.

Apparent is the luminescent glimmer

that dulls the phosphorescent tract lighting,

and cradles our conversation.

Our lips move, lick, purse and smile.

And this moment is laughing at having given us

an awareness

that we are blind

and so envied for it.

And in our talk,

our meld of voices,

a spark-wheel splinters flint

exploding into flame,

and the five temporarily go up in flames... as we laugh,

our eyes darting up and down each other like spotlights,

not knowing what to look for,

but illuminating all the right places.

The flames extinguish, the five return,

and the silence of the meeting

in the midst of the heartening laughter concludes.

And as the party separates,

deposits dishes, plastic utensils, and Styrofoam cups,

the glimmer remains as halos

we float out the cafeteria on.

PAPERCLIPS

Gentle peace and terrible hostility are acted out upon her knee by

the low buzzing 400-Watt heater at her side.

The burn through thin olive-green trousers is a slow stoking of dead

wood covered in tar... burning faster, hotter, and longer.

The single-celled (?) organism within her, a copper coil in glass that

doesn't waver, is not selective in its prey.

It devours the air and space between silence without jealousy or

bigotry.

It does not care.

She has fallen and is picking herself up, by the jutting shoulder

blades, off "Charity Street."

The faces of dead authors have been burned into her skull, and the

beat of still drums, like children, cost her more than she will believe.

There is an Egyptian exhibit being held down the side of last night's

street where all the bandaged souls and paupers wield hot brands.

There are tattered hieroglyphics and the scent of mercury and trees

being sold in gathered cloisters of onlookers, secretly praying,

wrapped in hemp ribbons and English bums.

Saffron.

Sage.

Sacrilege.

Sandal-feet men bind themselves backward with knotted wire and

tallow caked nails.

They whisper and tap their needle-like toes on the sun-baked street

like an impossible Morse Code from one millipede to another.

The heater blows the fuse.

The house is caught mid-sentence with a choke.

He is there to pat it hard on the back.

He is there to help pick her up.

She has fallen, and now he is found walking down "Charity Street,"

only the opposite way...

the wrong way... the right way...

His way.

He grabs her slender elbow like the wings of a moth, delicate and

precise, before it is pinned to the matte.

He has fingers as thin as paperclips, and just as crooked.

He is not old; rather, farfetched and caught catching one too may

photographs in the dark.

She is not young, but her elbows are, and concede like the "First

Time," when she was on the bathroom floor, on cold linoleum, and

it was frantic and unplanned, not unwanted, but not sanctioned.

It was taken.

It was to be had.

It was.

And she rose.

The bottles of strange memories give way to the bandaged souls

and paupers.

They have made their peace, their cent.

They are not abused, simply swallowed and turning from the

clicking of toes, from the incendiary branding before their
gauze-

shielded eyes, from the scent of trees and mercury rising, and
find

they have been summoned again.

Somewhere else,

before ever being dismissed.

But now—

under the Pacific night

a star arch of dashboard

the ripe grape moon

we are together.

PRETENDING TO BUSY HIMSELF

the barometer clock

a grease proof bag

ripe fruit

water on the watercress

wasps at the beer bottles

wheezing armchair

lilac and flower beds

slightly goggling eyes

cycling without lights

behind blue flames

embellished with puppy dogs

threaded streams

deep red suited you best

candlelight on guests faces

still photography

aqueous world

pajama cord

press round ragged fashion

polished lavender

khaki shorts and knobby knees

satisfactory concession of circumstances

unsubtle old shark

shutter flicked

bomb damaged embankment

stout martyr

on morning headlines

corpulent man

victory cry

WRITERS' GROUP

A brilliant and full moon illuminates the world,

and carries melancholies like a child,

hidden in the starry sky from a raging, fiery lover,

who again slammed the door, with a cascade of sunset,

locking the night in behind.

It's only the writers' group,

in the middle of a cold, cloudless winter.

Again, no one is on time,

but everyone is more than there.

The hostess is barefoot,

and every movement like a dance,

her coiled springs of autumn hair migrate

up and down and across her speckled ivory neck.

We expect nothing less,

her lips describing years of life

and of incomprehensible loss in this city.

Cats mewl, skulk and settle in to watch,

shifty-eyed from the nooks of the room.

The poets, rhymers, dreamers, escapists and journalists

settle into pockets of futon, planes of hardwood,

mitts of suede or faux-leather,

as word bubbles appear,

balloon from their mouths,

hover over their heads,

and float off into the night.

Only the cats truly see this.

The gay man gesticulates and laughs,

as if he is doing some naughty, or again wants to.

He whose words move in and out of humor and sincerity

like a slalom skier, coming close, but never brushing the wavering poles;

like a tennis player whose every riposte is too near to tell if it is over or under the out.

The Asian girl's legs crisscross, her gaze,

distracting enough to ever be pinned down,

looks into the abstract, Eternity and Afterlife,

with a cloudy mirror.

She holds hands with herself,

and if love is to come from some Where, some Place,

it comes on the soles of her shoes,

leaving heart-shaped footsteps on the floor.

The straight boy, reading the poem now,

brows furrow like a writer,

like a plagiarist studying another's lies,

taking notes for his own lines,

who never notices the gay man's tone, hard muscles,

his flirtatious, mischievous eyes,

the way he has worked his body into something good,

Who never notices the Asian girl's thin wrists,

her charming way of pursing every laugh,

starting and ending every gift with outstretched arms,

Who never places the hostess's portraits,

queer Madeleine L'Englian *Wind in the Door* caricatures,

her affinity for touching her apologies to her lips.

The straight boy, reading the poem right now,

shifts his posture, wipes, raises his right hand,

and brings his thumb to middle finger,

"SNAPS," his finish.

BLUR OF THE DIM

Since you will no longer

rise like a coffin in a vacuum

tube like the oxygen mask

strapped to the drunk

monoxide surgeon I welcome

you aboard this flight

into nowhere.

Pumps on-line and pressure resuming

zero or perhaps a halo

or a descent back into the land

of the living who congregate

in Guatemala City after an ex-

plosion. Pina Coladas and hot women

at this range may kill

you dead. When I saw you, I knew

how easy it would be.

All it took was the guess

of a Canadian named "Frenchy."

I snap pictures and number the contact

sheet with letters. I offer a fair price

and barely break even.

So, I suppose your innocence

was spared like dolphins upon the open

sea. The entire experience is reversed

regurgitated street lamps and reflections

inhaled as you'd cough on

sweets looking between your legs

for a gun. Suffering pitch withdrawal.

I can live every article in its prime.

When at times the expanse of a life-

time spreads like bread without butter

or terror without bliss, I dispose belief,

go ballistic in a magnificent hoodoo

of extremes that play the soul like

a hooker bobbing up and down, but I couldn't

believe a moment. Your truth. It's coming,

the smear of tears and darkness

from casted shadows of candlelight

and Avenues labeled "Rues."

We are single. We are peoples

parted and clawing at abandonment

like parked cars resisting a glove;

limitless and potentially restricted.

To not run away when you can,

when you should. Every vision delivered in

its time is lucid and informal like a tooth

pulled free resting in a dish

with a swish of blood

and lust, saliva, mixing

the monuments of destination,

ending, penetrating. Extremities.

I in my own arms play pretend

and they are yours with lips that

kiss and defame truth

inside a paper bag and POP!

You will be identified by

moments of signature like your hand held

cocked, of debits,

of wrinkles and scars of the skin.

Ah, whole impending benediction lost!

Arresting this suction or intake of ex-

plosive genius harbored in blue

x-rays like a lake, a lagoon, void of tide

and touch and distant murmurs.

I examine the emptiness and

condemn myself.

The jury is a slap.

RESTLESS

Slender gaps in the blinds

Betray, inviting the moonlight,

Gathering on ivory skin as milk.

Tiny rivulets converge,

Stream between her breasts,

Pool around her navel.

Rising distant

From a dream, body adrift

Among sheets instead of waves.

Struggles over white-capped crests,

Descends, settling in a wound

That never has fully healed.

THE SPACES BETWEEN

At one point in our relationship

I thought that I had touched you.

At one point I actually thought I had penetrated,

pushed deep inside you and massaged your tender heart.

It was that day we traded in what we wore

for who we are and bathed together for the first time.

Our bodies are made of many molecules,

and surprisingly enough, the spaces between

the coagulated proton and neutron soup,

and its singular or multiple orbiting electrons,

in even the minimalist of examples,

is greater than the distance of the earth from the moon.

We are more made of space than not,

and if I wished hard enough, I could reach through your flesh,

through your heart,

and out your back,

before you ever noticed that you had not been touched.

www.ingramcontent.com/pod-product-compliance
Lightning Source LLC
Chambersburg PA
CBHW051739040426

42447CB00008B/1216